Copyright © 2017 Lisa A. Person

All rights reserved.

ISBN-10: 1985158590
ISBN-13: 978-1985158597

DEDICATION

This book is dedicated to all women, young and mature. My desire is that after reading this book you truly know that you are a gift from God. I pray that you embrace the fact that there is nothing you can do or not do to stop God from loving you. You are perfect in His eyes. He loves you no matter what you have or have not done. He loved you before you were formed in your mother's womb and He loves you now. He loved you so much that He gave the life of His only begotten son that whosoever believes shall not perish but have everlasting life (John 3:16). Make Jesus the Lord of your life and come back into fellowship with your Father if you have not been connected to Him recently. Run to Him as He pursues you with His love constantly. God will give you beauty for ashes. No matter what you have been through, God only sees you as his beautiful daughter, the apple of His eye.

INTRODUCTION

The reason I am writing this book is because I want every woman to know God loves us. He loves every single one of us more than we can think or imagine. His love will provide us the strength to demand fair and equal treatment in this world. We deserve equal pay for equal work. We deserve to not be objectified or harassed by men or women. We deserve to be treated with respect in all situations at all times. Our Father in Heaven intends for us to be a doorway to Him not a doormat for anyone. We need to be united and be strong.

Our lives have a purpose to serve the Lord Jesus and to serve each other. Our purpose is not found in money, houses, cars, clothes, or shoes. Things provide only temporary satisfaction and have no bearing on that which God has called us to do. Our lives have a purpose not found in the arms of a man or woman, please realize that. Past hurts can blind us to that fact. The emptiness we may sometimes feel can be filled by no man or woman, because God put that space there to reserve his place in our hearts. He wants us to seek Him and His purpose for us. We must all open our hearts to Jesus and receive His saving grace. He is waiting with open arms to receive you and me, no matter the time or the place. I pray this book will be a blessing to you by reminding you of God's unconditional, unfailing love. I also pray this book will move you to action to make this world a better place for all women!

TABLE OF CONTENTS

	Acknowledgments	1
1	Always be yourself.	3
2	There will always be people that do not like you.	10
3	Expand your mind. Read more.	14
4	Fear not.	18
5	Do not define yourself through things.	23
6	Take your eyes off yourself and find yourself.	27
7	Take I can't out of your vocabulary.	30
8	I believe you can do anything, but you must believe in yourself.	33
9	Focus on your future. It is coming whether you are prepared or not.	36
10	Wisdom is a necessity.	39

ACKNOWLEDGMENTS

I want to dedicate this book to all of the amazing women who have guided me, mentored me, believed in me, befriended me, and loved me over the course of my life. I have been blessed to have many women who helped me through life, through school, throughout my career, and through the many hard times that life may bring. Each one of you know who you are. Thank you so much for taking the time to care about and help another woman achieve more in life. I can never repay you but I will continue to sow those same seeds in the lives of other women!

I want to thank my prayer partner and confidant, my best friends, my sisters in love vs. blood, and my birth sister, as well as my stepsister. I want to thank my mother-in-love and my stepdaughter for their support. I also want to thank my mom and my aunt for their love. This book is dedicated to my grandmother, Lucille Wilkerson, who guided me throughout my life until her passing when I was 24 years old. Lucy, as she was affectionately called, or grandma to me, was a woman with very limited formal education but could help me with my school work all the way through high school. She never attended seminary but knew the bible as well as anyone I have ever met. She served in the church and loved her family. She taught me the meaning of unconditional love and she set my life on a path for success.

Grandma was very soft spoken but did speak her mind. She supported my every dream and let me know all things are possible through Christ. I am sure her prayers sustained me throughout my teenage years and young adult life. My grandma was very special to me and I am sure many of you have or had a similar relationship with your grandmas. This book is dedicated to my grandma but is also dedicated to your "Lucy" if you were blessed to have someone, any woman, show you unconditional love.

1 Always be yourself.

We live in a world where very few things are really as they seem. Women have body altering surgeries to appear to be something that they are not because of the body image and beauty pressures of society. Men sexually harass and assault women and lie about it to continue to hold positions of power. Politicians (all parties) lie for points in the polls. We have wars for reasons that many of us don't understand. We still have people who hate us, as Americans, waiting for another opportunity to kill us by the thousands. We no longer identify a clear right and wrong in many instances in society. Everything is grey in many people's minds. No matter what your view of the world may be, there are definites. One definite is that every person will ask themselves "Who am I" at some point in life.

Some people seem to know and understand themselves from birth and others take decades to figure out the answer to who we are. If you are someone who is in the process of defining yourself, let me comfort you. Very few people truly know who they are even if they seem to have it all together. I know more about myself than ever before, but I am still in the process. The bottom line is that finding out who you are requires answering a series of questions not just that one. Also, as long as you are alive, you are hopefully continuing to change and grow as a person.

To figure out who we are now, we must all ask ourselves a series of questions. Each of us must find out the answers to: who created me, what is my purpose in life, what are my core beliefs, and what does all of this mean as far as how I relate to the people and the world around me.

Who created me? God intentionally made each of us unique individuals. God purposefully made you just as you are. You are not flawless, but you are perfect because God made you in His image (Genesis 1:26).

What is my purpose in life? There is something God created you to do and nobody else can fulfill that purpose. Don't compare yourself or your life to others. You are special and unique. God knew you before He formed you in your mother's womb (Jeremiah 1:5). God numbered every hair on your head (Matthew 10:30). He knows every freckle on your face. He has studied each and every one of us. We are all fearfully and wonderfully made (Psalm 139:14). It is a freeing revelation to know that all of the things that people call "quirks", and all of the things that people consider "ugly", "unattractive", "unpopular" were all fearfully and wonderfully made a part of you. You are who you are on purpose. You have a Lord in heaven who has a purpose for you and He gave you the personality you have to fulfill that purpose. He gave you the physical body and face that you have purposefully and wonderfully.

Build your self-image through the eyes of God not the eyes of man. Only God is your creator. Only God knows your purpose. Seek God and He will tell you what your purpose in life is. God is constant. His love is not fleeting. The love and admiration of man is fleeting and many people tell you that. However, few will tell you that the hatred and disdain of man is also fleeting. Don't allow a few people's lack of knowledge to affect you. Moments of hurt and rejection will pass and your life must continue. You will be an adult much longer than you will ever be a child or teenager. Don't allow the formative years to be a negative in your life. No matter when you experience rejection in your life, don't let that period of hurt or rejection define you. God loves you. Discover His purpose for you by spending time in His word.

What are my core beliefs? One of my core beliefs is that God loves me and Jesus Christ died for my sins to reconcile me with my Father who loves me. I have received Jesus Christ into my life and my heart as my personal Lord and Savior. Jesus Christ is Lord and loved me so much that he was crucified and resurrected three days later just for me and just for you. As a Christian, God sees me through the blood of Jesus, so I am perfect in His eyes, not because of anything that I do but because of who I know (Jesus). This does not mean that I should sin and fall short consistently, but if I do, there is a God who loves me and will forgive me if I repent in the name of Jesus. He does that for you also. Therefore, we don't have to live under condemnation (Romans 8:1), but instead we can leave the past behind and press on to the higher calling. Your past does not dictate your future unless you allow it to do so.

Another of my core beliefs is that God loves all of us. Almighty God loves you. Almighty God loves me. Because God loves us and we are His children, He wants us to love ourselves and see ourselves as He sees us. I did not always allow myself to see me as God sees me. I spent much of my teenage years being extremely self-conscious and feeling like I did not measure up. I moved from living with my grandparents as a baby and young child to living with my parents. Once that happened, I did not receive encouragement at home. My household was one that believed in negative motivation. I did not get pep talks when I failed or get assistance to help me succeed. I did not fit in with everyone at school. I did not have the newest clothes. I was shy and felt awkward for a very long time. I felt like I could never be pretty enough, nice enough, popular enough, smart enough, or successful enough. However, all of these negative thoughts were on the surface versus deeply held beliefs because I had grandparents who at a very early age taught me that God loves me unconditionally. Once I went back to that core belief and found my way back to the Word of God and the love of God, those negative voices were silenced. God loves and adores us. He loves me just as I am, and He loves you and adores you as you are. My prayer is that you let God's love silence the negative thoughts you have of yourself.

What does all this mean as far as how I relate to the people and the world around me? This means always be yourself. In every circumstance and situation be confident in who you are. Remember that God who loves you made you fearfully and wonderfully, and He wants you to love yourself. So, Love yourself!! Be confident. Love the things you think are good about you and the things you think are bad about you. God made you as you are to fulfill a purpose only you can fulfill. Seek the Lord to find out your purpose. Once you know why you are here, everything else in your life will fall into place. You will more clearly be able to answer who you are. You will embrace your purpose and yourself and move forward with the Lord with all your heart, mind, soul, and strength. Always be yourself!

Famous Quotes:

I don't care what you think about me. I don't think about you at all. – Coco Chanel

I think the reward for conformity is that everyone likes you except yourself. – Rita Mae Brown

Success is liking yourself, liking what you do, and liking how you do it. – Maya Angelou

In order to always be yourself, you must first know yourself. You must find the answers to life's questions for you as a woman, as your own unique person created by God. My journey to knowing who I am, what my purpose in life is, and how I relate to the world around me has been a long and complex journey. I lived with my grandparents during my formative years. They were both amazing people. We were poor and actually lived in a trailer on a few acres in the mountains of West Virginia. However, they loved me (and my brother). They taught me the Word of God and took me to church every Sunday. I did not know at that time how important that love and training in the Lord would be later in life. As young as I can remember, my grandparents engrained in me a sense of self through the love of the Lord. Although my life, especially my youth, had its ups and downs, I never stopped believing in God. I have always known I was chosen by God and created in His image. I have definitely had some growing pains and still have times where I need to recalculate my goals and objectives in life to keep moving forward in God's purpose. I even allowed negative thoughts to shake my self-image for a period in my life but because of the foundation my grandparents gave me, I never questioned my value as a woman. I always knew my life was bought with a price more precious than all of the money of the world. My life was bought through the blood of Jesus the Christ. However, I had to grow and develop an understanding of me as a person and what my unique calling in life is. I now know God has called me to help others. I know God has given me a heart for people. I know God has chosen me to be a blessing to His children in any way He allows me to do so. I know that my life is not about me but about who God can help through me. I know I am loved beyond measure and blessed beyond bounds. Finally, I know my circumstances whether good or bad are just temporary. This life is but a whiff and the most important thing I know is that I will answer to God one day and give an account for how I have spent my days on this earth. I know that when I stand before Him, I want to be able to say that I helped others with a right heart in your name Lord and I will say that I was always myself, the self you made me to be God. What will you say?

2 There will always be people that do not like you.

Have you ever walked in a room and gotten the distinct feeling that some of the people in the room don't like you. At first, you think maybe you are being self-conscious, but then it is confirmed by a look or a harsh word that some people in the room have formed an opinion of you before you even had a chance to say a word to them. As women, we do that a lot to each other. Many of us decide we don't like another female just because of how she looks, or how she walks, or because of the attention she gets from men that we may want. This is something that speaks to the self-image of many women, but it also lets us all know that there will always be people that do not like us. Please don't misunderstand me. We have all given some people a reason not to like us, but more often than not you will encounter people who you don't have to give a reason. They just don't like you or me. Over the years, I have realized that there will always be people that do not like you. Those people do not have to like you, but your response to their dislike will determine whether or not they have to respect you and whether or not you have respect for yourself. Learn to hold your head high (without being prideful) and carry on.

Many times when people don't like us, our pride is hurt. It is our pride that will make us want to fight someone who says something to us that is mean. Our pride is what makes us want to cuss someone who does something that we think is rude. Our pride will cause us to make stupid decisions that can have far-reaching, negative consequences in our life. Please don't be deceived, pride is not the core of having a positive self-image. The love of God is the core of having a positive self-image. Pride is not pleasing to God. God's word says that "In the mouth of the foolish is a rod of pride" (Psalm 14:3). Do not let pride and ego drive your decisions. Most of the time, prideful decisions are foolish decisions. Ask God to help you control your pride and He will do just that. Then, you will realize that it is possible to not respond harshly to people who don't like you. You may even find yourself being kind to them. Always remember that it is easy to show love to those that love you, but the true test is whether you can show love to those that despise you. The Lord says "recompense to no man evil for evil…vengeance is mine…overcome evil with good" (Romans 12:17-21).

Famous Quotes:

You don't have to like everybody but you have to

love everybody. - Fannie Lou Hamer

I do not trust people who don't love themselves and yet tell me, "I love you." There is an African saying which is: Be careful when a naked person offers you a shirt. – Maya Angelou

You can't please everyone and you can't make everyone like you. – Katie Couric

If you just set out to be liked, you would be prepared to compromise on anything at any time, and you would achieve nothing." – Margaret Thatcher

Throughout my life, there have been people that did not like me and I knew it. There have also been people I trusted that have betrayed me, and as it turns out really did not like me at all. There have been people that barely knew me that did not like me. Most hurtful, have been the people that have spread lies about me. I went through many responses to these people and the situations they created in my life. At one stage in my life, I would lose sleep if I thought someone did not like me. As a teenager, I became hard-hearted and could care less what people thought or said about me. Then, the Lord brought balance into my life. You must be well-balanced to have peace in your life. This is what the Lord spoke to me:

Be yourself. Love those that love you and love those that hate you. Don't be a doormat. Be a doorway to me. Do not let other peoples' opinions of you or words about you become your opinion of yourself. Know that hurting people hurt people. Have mercy on them as I have for you. Forgive them and love them as I love you.

I hope the words that Jesus spoke to me can help you in your life.

3 Expand your mind. Read more.

Often, we as women feel like we are in a "rut". As I have matured, I have realized that all of my "ruts" started in my mind. Changing your mind will change your life. Romans 12:2 says be ye transformed by the renewing of your mind. Learning new things renews your mind, body, and soul. All of us must try new things to grow as a people. If you never take advantage of new opportunities to learn, and new challenges, you will never know what life has to offer. You will settle for less than the destiny God intends for you. Expand your mind. We must spend as much time on our inner-beauty as we do our outer-beauty. Reading is an excellent way to expand your mind. Frederick Douglas said "Once you learn to read, you will be forever free."

Have you ever heard that as a man thinketh in his heart, so is he (Proverbs 23:7). Reading can change your life because it will change your thoughts. Your thought life drives the words you speak. The words you speak drive your actions. Your actions develop your character. Your character is the foundation of your life, your destiny.

My favorite book to read is the Holy Bible. Through reading the Bible, I have learned that the majority of positive books are derivatives of some part of the Bible. I have not read every book that people consider a classic. I can't quote the most popular authors of the day. However, I have read books that have changed my life. The book of Genesis let me know that I was made in the image of my Almighty God and I am not a descendant of an ape. The book of Jeremiah let me know that my Lord knew me before he formed me in my mother's womb. The Psalms taught me how to pray to God. Proverbs taught me that wisdom is the principle thing. The book of Hebrews let me know that there is no such thing as reincarnation (Hebrew 9:27). Other books in The New Testament of the Bible taught me that I am to live a victorious, joyful, and peaceful life because I have a Lord who came so that I may have life and have it more abundantly (John 10:10). The word of God says that I am to prosper and be in health even as my soul prospers (3 John 1:2). Most importantly, I learned that I am saved from an eternity in hell because I have received Jesus Christ as my Lord and Savior (Romans 10:9-13). What a joy to know that God cares about every aspect of our life. The Holy Bible is a book that I highly recommend you read. It is my favorite book but I have read many other books over the course of my life. I enjoy studying black history. I enjoy reading self-help books many of which are derivatives of some teaching of the bible. I enjoy reading books about leadership and business. I am not advocating that you limit your reading to the Bible only, but I am advocating that you include the Bible in your reading list.

The purpose of reading should be to gain wisdom that will change you, to find a part of you that you did not know was there or that you thought you lost, to grow as a person, to understand something that was confusing, to expand your thinking, and to know the Lord. To know God, you must read His Word. To have wisdom, you must know God. A well-read person has information. An intelligent person has wisdom and understanding gained through information .

Read more. It will change your life.

Famous Quotes:

There are many little ways to enlarge your child's world. Love of books is the best of all. – Jacqueline Kennedy

Any book that helps a child to form a habit of reading, to make reading one of his needs, is good for him. – Maya Angelou

My grandmother taught me to read before I was three years old. She fostered a love of reading in my life before I ever started school. By the fifth grade, I was winning reading contests for reading the most books in a year in my class and I was reading encyclopedias for fun. That early effort by my grandmother to ensure I loved to read laid a path for success in my life. It is true that leaders are readers. Reading changed my life and it will change your life and the life of your children.

4 Fear not.

Have you ever been afraid, flat out petrified by something or someone? I had all kinds of fear in my life at different stages of life. I was afraid of talking in front of a group of people. I was afraid of failing, so I would not try new things. I was afraid of death. I was afraid of the people I love dying. I was afraid of not being able to pay the bills. My list can go on and on. I have realized that fear is false evidence appearing real. Fear is crippling. Fear will stop you and me from living and enjoying our lives. Fear is one of the most powerful emotions. Most of the time we fear things that never come to pass and even if it does come to pass it is not as bad as we made it in our minds. Removing fear from my life gave me a new life. I realized that I really was not living before. I was just existing. Fear is not of God. Fear not!!

The word of God says perfect love casteth out all fear (I John 4:18). Fear is not a natural part of us regardless of what doctors and scientists say. You are not born with a fear of heights, falling, or loud noises. All fear is developed and comes into our lives as a trick of the devil. If the devil can get you to have fear in your life, he can get you to make decisions based in fear and take you down a path you don't want to go.

However, he will make you think you want to go there and that you are a horrible person once you are there. Know this, the devil is a liar. He is the father of lies (John 8:44). Satan is a liar from the pits of hell. You are not to live by fear, you are to live by faith. Faith is the substance of things hoped for, the evidence of things not yet seen (Hebrews 11:1).

God loves you. He is love. He protects you and has mercy on you. Because of His great love for you and me, He gives each of us a measure of faith (Romans 12:3) that is enough to overcome any fear. We are to walk by that faith and not by sight (2 Corinthians 5:7). However, you must receive Jesus Christ as the Lord of your life in order to truly walk by faith, drive out fear even the fear of death, and receive the promises of God. Make the most important decision of your life today. Receive Jesus into your heart. Simply say God, I have sinned against you, and I repent. I ask for your forgiveness. I believe that Jesus lived a sinless life, died on the cross for my sins, and rose again three days later. I receive you, Jesus, as my Lord and Savior right now. Come and live in my heart. Once you have prayed this prayer, you may instantly feel a change and you may not. Regardless, you are now a Christian. If you don't feel changed, you can ask the Lord to reveal himself to you. Jesus will come to you just as He came to me one day laying on my couch. I asked him to prove that He is real and He did. I have never been the same, and neither will you. Once you have received Jesus, you will truly be able to live by faith, faith that God loves you and will keep you, and faith that all things work together for good for those that love God (Romans 8:28).

Faith is the opposite of fear. Fear is faith in the devil and the lies that he tells you. Faith is trust in the Lord and His promises. You must learn to trust in the Lord with all your heart and lean not to your own understanding. Trusting in the Lord is a way to exercise your faith. God promises that if you delight in Him, He will give you the desires of your heart (Psalm 37:4). God cares about every aspect of your life from the smallest to the largest. You do not have to fear anything. God will heal your body if you ask Him and believe His word which says that by Jesus' stripes you were healed (Isaiah 53:5). God will take care of your children and family. God will take care of your finances (Phil 4:19). God will remove loneliness from your heart. He is the friend that sticks closer than a brother (Proverbs 18:24). God will protect you and your family and loved ones (Psalm 91). God will deliver you from strongholds and sin (Galatians 5:1). Rest in the peace of putting your trust in your Creator. God promises us a peace that passes all understanding (Phil 4:7). Have faith in God and His promises. Look up by subject in the Holy Bible the things you want or need from God and stand on what His word promises you. Whatever is going on in your life, God has a word for you. He can make you whole. Fear not! You have a Lord who loves you and has overcome the world so that you can live without fear.

Famous Quotes:

Knowing what must be done does away with fear. – Rosa Parks

The most difficult thing is the decision to act. The rest is merely tenacity. – Amelia Earhart

You can waste your lives drawing lines or you can live your life crossing them. – Shonda Rhimes

Fear is not something you overcome one time. Fear is something that you push through daily. For me, I confront fear head on. I have found that if I let fear linger, it becomes stronger and stronger. Fear in my life can arise about family, finances, fear of failure and the list goes on but I have learned to trust God. Trusting Him means that I know God loves me. I am His daughter. He wants only the best for me. Why should I fear when my Daddy owns all things and is in control of all things. If God is for me, who can be against me (Romans 8:31). No weapon formed against me shall prosper (Isaiah 54:17). He is your daddy too. We are all joint heirs to the throne. You are royalty!!! Fear not my queen!

5 Do not define yourself through things.

We live in a world where the majority of people define themselves through things. Even people who are saying with their words that they don't define themselves through things show with their actions that they really do.

When two people want to get to know each other, one of the first questions they ask is what do you do. We rarely ask someone what are your beliefs or what charities do you support with your time, talents, and money. Most often we want to know how you make a living to buy things.

We idealize celebrities and their things. Everyone seems to want to portray an image of having it all. Social media has made this phenomenon even worse. People post moments in time and try to show things in the best possible light to create an image. Things are always front and center in most posts. When people try to appear to live a life of all fun and money, or try to appear that they have the best relationship ever created, or try to appear to live a life of no stress just blessed with stuff, it breeds a poisonous appetite for more and more things.

Young people see image after image of wealthy people living extravagant lives. Who would not want that as it is portrayed. What they don't show is the inner turmoil and lack of fulfillment that many people who chase things live. We don't hear the stories of people who seemed to have it all, but killed themselves or have drug addictions, or bounce from spouse to spouse because they are looking to fill an emptiness that only God can fill.

If things can make you happy, why do we keep developing and buying new things. If you try to define yourself by inanimate objects, you will find that you don't have much definition in your life at all. Things provide a temporary high, a temporary sense of fulfillment that is fleeting. Please understand that God intends for His children to be wealthy and prosper. He intends for us to live comfortably and yes even in luxury. However, we are to prosper and be in health even as our soul prospers (3 John 1:2). In that scripture, Jesus is letting us know that if our soul is not at peace and prospering, no thing will be enough. Do not define yourself through things because you will never have peace. Define yourself through Jesus, the Peace Maker, the giver of peace.

Jesus calls us to love our neighbor as ourselves, care for each other, give to the poor, not live self-centered, self-serving, selfish lives. We are to give and it will be given unto us in good measure pressed down shaken together and running over. Use the blessings that God has given you whether you are rich or poor to be a blessing to others beyond the four walls of your home. You will be amazed at how fulfilled you will be. You will receive more satisfaction from sharing with others than you ever will from buying another thing. Things are often an external show to impress others. Cars and homes bring fleeting happiness but the opportunity to help and impact the life of another person, another of God's children will never leave your soul.

Do not define yourself through things. Define yourself through the Word of God. Be blessed to be a blessing, not to be a show-off.

Jesus gave us two commandments (Matthew 22:37-40). Love the Lord your God with all your heart, mind, soul, and strength; and love your neighbor as you love yourself. If you define your existence according to these commandments, you will find righteousness, peace, and joy through loving God. You will find fulfillment through loving others.

Famous quotes:

Human greatness does not lie in wealth or power,

but in character and goodness. People are just people, and all people have faults and shortcomings, but all of us are born with basic goodness. – Anne Frank

You can only become truly accomplished at something you love. Don't make money your goal. Instead, pursue the things you love doing, and then do them so well that people can't take their eyes off you. – Maya Angelou

I want to clarify that I have nice things but they do not define me. I buy the homes, cars, clothes, shoes, and jewelry that I like and that God has blessed me to be able to afford but I also donate more than 10% of my gross income to charity. I give of my time to other people and causes in which I believe. I feel no different in a $30 pair of shoes than I do in a $1500 pair of shoes. I say this to say it is great to have nice things that you like if you can afford them but they do not define us. Our Father in heaven and our relationship with him defines us. He says we are beautiful in His eyes!

6 Take your eyes off yourself and find yourself.

The bible says that he who finds his life will surely lose it and he who loses his life for Jesus and the sake of the gospel will surely find it (Luke 17:33). Life sometimes feels like a game of hide and seek. You are in a constant journey to find yourself as you grow and change. As you search to find yourself know that there is a confident, strong, successful, happy, joyful woman inside you. That is the person that God created. That is the person you will one day be when you realize who you are because of whose you are. You are God's child. Your earthly parents are your caregivers chosen by God, but your identity comes through God not earthly things, just as your purpose comes from God.

Many of us believe now or at least at one time in our lives believed that our happiness, our level of success, our essence is defined through things. In our current society, money has become a substitute for character and integrity. We totally excuse and ignore horrendous behavior because a person has achieved wealth. We have become a society fixated on things and not on purpose of life or character of the person. Go against the norm! Find and chase God's purpose for your life vs. material things. Take your eyes off yourself and the things you think you want. You will be far more blessed when you lose yourself, your earthly desire to pursue things, and find yourself in God's purpose which always includes helping others.

Famous Quotes:

Service is the rent you pay for room on this earth. – Shirley Chisholm

Whenever you are blue or lonely or stricken by some humiliating thing you did, the cure and the hope is in caring about other people." – Diane Sawyer

I have learned that people will forget what you said, people will forget what you did, but people will never forget how you made them feel. – Maya Angelou

Please understand that I am not saying you should not take care of yourself or think of yourself at all. I am not advocating that any woman be a doormat. I am simply saying set out to also have a purpose in life that includes helping others beyond your home. Set out to be a blessing by not being subsumed with self. It is so easy in this society to only think of ourselves and what we need or want. However, there is always someone more in need than us. There is always someone hurting more than us. There is always someone lonelier, in more financial trouble, or sicker than us. If we take our eyes off of ourselves, God can use us to help others.

7 Take I can't out of your vocabulary.

Can't is one of the most powerful words in the English language and we use is so cavalierly that it is second nature for many to say "I can't". If you take nothing else from this section of the book please take this point – remove "I can't" from your vocabulary.

When you say I can't you are saying that there is no hope. If you say I can't and lose hope, you will quit before you start. The Word of God says hope deferred makes the heart sick (Proverbs 13:12). Don't quit. There is always hope. You must be full of hope. Where would we be today if Rev. Martin Luther King Jr. had said "I can't'? or the Freedom Fighters had quit? or if Abraham Lincoln had said "I can't"? or if Barack Obama had not said "yes we can" or if George Washington had given up during the Revolutionary War? Most people never walk in their destiny not for lack of ability, but for lack of fortitude. "I can't" will rob you of your destiny.

Always look at yourself with optimism. Be hopeful about your future. Believe that you can do anything that you discipline yourself to do. You can do all things through Christ which strengthens you (Phil 4:13).

Learn to talk positively to yourself. We talk to ourselves more than anyone else. Make your self-talk positive. Write positive affirmations that you read to yourself and you will see a dramatic change in your attitude and actions. Dump the junk from your mind and make room for new thoughts. Take "I can't" out of your mind and mouth and replace it with hope. Hope does not disappoint us (Romans 5:5).

Famous Quotes:

Every time you state what you want or believe, you are the first to hear it. It's a message to both you and others about what you think is possible. Don't put a ceiling on yourself. – Oprah Winfrey

Don't listen to those who say you can't. Listen to the voice inside yourself that says, I can. – Shirley Chisholm

I have found that the greatest blessings in my life have come from trying to do the things that I or others thought I could not do. When that little negative voice in my head said "I can't" but I did it anyway, I have always found a blessing on the other side. I never thought I could be a member of the senior executive service (SES) in the Federal government. I thought I can't because I am too young (at the time) or because I am a black female, or because any number of negative thoughts. However, I knew I could work hard, learn fast and be the best me I could be. As others believed in me, I believed more in myself and turned "I can't" into "I can". I did become a member of the senior executive service where blacks are still less than 12% of the total percentage of SESs. The same was true when I was working to pay my way through college, when buying my first home, when marrying the man of my dreams, and on and on. If you press through when that little voice says "I can't", you will realize that yes you can!

8 I believe you can do anything, but you must believe in yourself.

In order to have success in life, you must believe in yourself. Believing in yourself is not wishful thinking as many want us to think. Believing in yourself is confident expectancy that what you are striving toward will come to be. You must believe that you will fulfill God's purpose for your life. You will succeed.

Success is not measured by dollars only. God wants all of his children to have success and to prosper, but my success may be different than your success. Success is fulfilling the call of God, whatever that may be. For some of us, God has called us to write. Others God has called to teach. Others have been called as pastors. Wealth is not the measure of success. Fulfillment of God's purpose for your life is the true measure of success. If you are not truly fulfilled, you are not walking in your destiny.

You will not walk in your destiny until you believe in yourself. Other people believing in you will be of no effect if you do not believe in yourself. Have you ever wondered why some people have no success, some have moderate success, and some have great success? Many people say it is luck. Some say it is a result of opportunity and preparedness meeting. I am confident it is a function of belief. Belief and faith are partners. You must have faith to believe and you must believe to have faith. I know belief in God, Jesus, and ourselves is critical to success. God said it is impossible to please Him without faith (Hebrews 11:6). If we do not have faith, we don't believe. We achieve the level of success we truly believe we can have not necessarily the level of success we want unless the two are the same. What do you truly believe? If you believe you can achieve it, you will.

Famous Quotes:

With every experience, you alone are painting your own canvas, thought by thought, choice by choice. – Oprah Winfrey

Optimism is the faith that leads to achievement. – Helen Keller

Life is a process that begins with your mind, your thought process. For me, I did not always have the right thought process. When you grow up with almost every type of dysfunction in your family, you tend to have some negative thinking to overcome. It took me well into my adult years to truly believe in myself. Please know that I always loved myself because I have always known who my Father in Heaven is but I did not always believe in myself. I spent years wanting to believe in myself, praying to believe in myself, and even having periods of time where I did believe in myself. However, it was not until I truly surrendered my life to the Lord and believed that He has a plan for my life that no man can stop that I believed in myself. My belief in myself came from knowing that I have a God who loves me and perfects all that concerns me (Psalm 138:8). You see, doubt in myself came from trying to do things in my own power, from thinking I have to be perfect to get a desired outcome. That is impossible, not true, and tiring. I believe in myself now because I truly believe that my Father in Heaven has a plan for my life. For I know the plans I have for you, declares the Lord, plans to prosper you and not to harm you, plans to give you hope and a future (Jeremiah 29:11).

9 Focus on your future. It is coming whether you are prepared or not.

Proverbs 29:18 says where there is no vision, the people perish. If you have no goals for your future, how do you plan to accomplish anything? I don't care how old you are, you should have personal, professional, and spiritual goals. If you have no vision for your life in mind, life will throw you for a loop. You will constantly go this way and that. As some say, you will go however the wind blows. Focus your energy. Focus your thoughts. Set goals and strive to achieve them. Your future is coming tomorrow.

If you fail to plan, you plan to fail. You just don't know it yet. Always have a plan. The Bible is clear that you are to write your vision upon tablets (Habakkuk 2:2). I have achieved every goal that I have ever written down and read back to myself. There is something about writing a goal that makes it become real to you. Goals in your head are really wishes. I believe a goal is not a goal until you write it down, think it through, meditate and pray on it. You should set short-term, intermediate, and long-term goals. Think them through and pray diligently. Make sure they are goals that are in line with God's purpose for your life. Then begin writing!!!

Famous quotes:

Without leaps of imagination or dreaming, we lose the excitement of possibilities. Dreaming after all is a form of planning. – Gloria Steinem

When we try to plan our future all the way to some long-term end, it can be overwhelming. Have a vision for your life and set goals but aim to achieve them one step at a time. Sometimes, you can only mentally fathom moving from point A to point B because moving from point A to point Z seems overwhelming. When starting a business, setting a goal to just be profitable (stay in the black) may be all you can plan for right now. My goal in business has always been to have clients with whom I enjoy working and stay in the black. As my business grows, I will set larger goals. In your career, being the CEO, CIO, CFO, or COO may be too much to imagine. I never imagined being a COO but I knew I learned quickly and I enjoyed the business of business. I always wanted to make things work more effectively and efficiently. So, I learned all I could about financial management, contracts, grants, human resources, strategic planning, project management, information technology, and facilities management. As I learned I was also promoted. Then, I learned and read more about leadership and management. I learned how to lead people as I learned the business of business. The more responsibility I was given the more I believed I could handle additional responsibility and leadership roles. I believed I could lead because I believed in the people and still believe in the people who choose to be a part of my teams. I also believed what my mentors told me about my abilities and followed their guidance throughout my career. It is truly people that make the world go round and make your visions a reality. It is also planning and work that will make your dreams come true. Start planning your future. Have a vision for your life, and just figure out how to get from point A to point B for now. Then, plan for point B to point C and on and on. Ensure your plans are in line with God's purpose and God will put the right people in your path to help you achieve your goals. I know you can have what you believe because our Father said so!!

10 Wisdom is a necessity.

Strive for wisdom. Wisdom is knowledge and understanding. Wisdom is not a memorization of facts with no context.

We have become a society of generalists in many regards and not even good generalists. We touch the surface of subjects with no real desire to truly understand, just a desire to appear to understand. Very few of us specialize in or pursue one subject that we come to know, understand, and have true wisdom about. Learn to study more and memorize less. Learn how to apply concepts vs. regurgitate facts.

"Happy is the woman who finds wisdom and the woman who gains understanding. For her proceeds are better than the profits of silver and her gain than fine gold. She is more precious than rubies and all the things you may desire cannot compare with her (Proverbs 3:13-15). The Lord and His word gives wisdom. Seek Him and find wisdom.

There is no short cut to wisdom. Wisdom is gained by experience and knowledge. Life experience gives us understanding and reading the Word of God and spending time with God gives us knowledge. As a teenager, I acted like I knew it all. As a twenty something, I knew I knew it all. In my thirties, I had no doubt I knew everything about everything. In my forties, I now realize how mistaken I was all those years. Socrates once said "the only true wisdom is in knowing you know nothing".

As the elders in my family have said to me, "live a little while and then tell me what you think". Well I have now lived just a little while and what I think is I have so much more to learn, but I am gaining more wisdom every day. I am learning that it is true experience is the best teacher but you can learn from the experience of others if you are willing to listen. I am learning not to sweat the small things. I am learning to appreciate the people I love every day. I am learning that when people show you who they are, believe them as Maya Angelou said. I am learning that barring a true change through the Lord, people do not really change that much. Do not for one minute think you can change somebody. I am learning to surround myself with positive, encouraging people. I am learning that if you have a couple of true friends, you should consider yourself blessed. I am learning that having true love is worth more than any amount of money in the world. I am learning that I need to love God first and most because He first loved me and He loves me more than any person can ever love me. I still have a lot to learn but I am gaining wisdom every day.

Famous Quotes:

Learn from the mistakes of others. You can't live long enough to make them all yourself. – Eleanor Roosevelt

Many receive advice. Only the wise profit from it. – Harper Lee

I want to give a special thank you to all of the women who have imparted wisdom to me over the course of my life. I want to thank every woman who sowed into my life spiritually, especially my prayer partner. I want to thank every woman who sowed kindness, love, and friendship into my life. I want to thank my closest friends (who are my sisters through love), my cousins (through birth and marriage), my aunts, my mom, my stepdaughter, my sister, my stepsister, my mother-in-love, my church family, and all of my mentors. You have helped me more than you can ever know. There is power in womanhood. There is a strength in our bonding, sharing , and helping each other. I love you and I thank you.

The woman I want to thank most for imparting wisdom to me is my grandmother, Lucille (Lucy) Wilkerson. Lucy was an amazing woman. She taught me so much. I remember her teaching me how to tie my shoes, how to put my little tights on for church, how to read, how to write, how to ride a bike, how to jump rope, how to dance, and how to try to sing. She supported me in cheerleading, in student government, in doing my homework. She loved me and taught me the love of a grandmother but also taught me the love of God. She loved the Lord with all her heart. She was the church treasurer and taught me math when balancing the church books. I knew how to add subtract, multiply, and divide before I ever started school. My grandmother barely had a high school education but she knew so much. She was wise and shared her wisdom with me. She knew what all women, especially black women in America, have to know. She knew how to take lemons and make lemonade, literally and figuratively.

She had a very difficult life but you would never know it. She was kind to everyone and through her I learned kindness. She judged nobody. I never heard her say a judgmental word about anyone. Through her, I learned to love everybody and help them if I can. She taught me how to fight fear. She was petrified to drive but I was in so many afterschool activities, she had to get her driver's license to chauffer me around when I was in the 5th grade. So, she passed her driving test with the help of my grandfather and we were off. My grandmother, my aunt, my cousin, and I were off to take on the big world of Long Branch, Mt. Hope, and Beckley West Virginia. When I came to live with my mother, who I love and appreciate so much, my grandmother overcame her fear of flying and would fly up to surprise me for a visit. Whenever I came home from school and she was there, it was better than Christmas. I would not leave her side. I wish each of you had the opportunity to know her but I am sure you had a "Lucy" in your life. If you have never had that special woman in your life, I pray God sends her to you because every woman needs that woman to guide you and teach you even if just for a short while.

My grandmother died when I was 24 years old and I felt like my heart was ripped out but I was still living. I think I was in a daze for at least 5 years after that. That period truly seems like a blur. I was not drunk or on drugs, although I do understand how that can happen when people are in that much pain. I was just there and nothing else. I missed her so much! I still miss her but all of her teachings from the Word of God came back to me and gave me peace. I know I have a purpose and I have to fulfill it. That purpose is to help others. I also know beyond a doubt that I will see my grandmother again in Heaven and when I do there will be no separating us. We will spend eternity in heaven together. Praise God for his love and mercy!! Thank you grandma for all of the wisdom you imparted in me!!

ABOUT THE AUTHOR

Lisa A. Person is a wife, a stepmother, a daughter, a friend, a sister, a mentor, and an aunt among many other things. She is an executive, a business owner, and an author. Above all else, Lisa is a child of the most high God and is a Christian who received Jesus as her Lord and Savior at a very young age. Lisa has a true desire to fulfill God's purpose to spread His love to all and to help all women know their true value by seeing themselves as the royalty they are created to be.

Made in the USA
Middletown, DE
30 May 2020